I0566927

ASK!
SEEK!
KNOCK!

MARY DONNA HANKLA

Mary Donna Hankla

Printed Worldwide
First Printing 2024
First Edition 2024

ISBN: 979-8-9880394-8-8

Library of Congress Control Number: 2024922122

10 9 8 7 6 5 4 3 2 1

Interior Book Design by Walt's Book Design
www.waltsbookdesign.com

Book Cover by Lou Designs @lgr202

All Scriptures used are from THE HOLY BIBLE, NEW
INTERNATIONAL VERSION®, NIV® Copyright © 1973,
1978, 1984, 2011 by Biblica, Inc.™

ASK!
SEEK!
KNOCK!

CONTENTS

DEDICATION

This book is written to inspire people to pray. Take time to ask, to seek and to knock.

I am grateful for intercessors who taught me to pray and inspired me to continue a lifestyle of prayer.

Kenneth Hankla is a loving and supportive husband. He stands with me in all ministry efforts. He always offers a helping hand.

Chris Hankla is the Computer Tech, who prepares the publishing aspects of the book. He is amazing with his skills, and he enjoys publishing books to encourage prayer.

My niece, Katrina Shefield, is a wonderful support. She encourages others to read these books.

Finally, I would like to dedicate this book to the faithful people of the Big 4 P.H. Church in Kimball, WV. Cecil Porterfield and Brenda Denton are faithful servants of God. Along with the other church members they encourage us to serve God with the publishing of books.

PRAYER LESSONS FROM THE OWL

The beauty of Nature provides inspiration. Taking hikes in the mountains is a way to relax and refresh. Just gazing at the mountains, the stars, and a sunset reminds us of the Majestic God!

"The heavens declare the glory of God; the skies proclaim the work of his hands. Day after day they pour forth speech; night after night they reveal knowledge." (Psalm 19: 1,2) (NIV)

Even Jesus went to the mountains to pray. (Mark 6:46)

I truly enjoy taking hikes into the mountains. In this serene atmosphere, I can sense God's Presence.

Often, I watch creatures in their natural habitat. Eagles, owls, deer, and other animals motivate me to pray, and to pursue God's Presence.

Owls have particularly fascinated me. When I was young, our family would sit out in the yard in the evenings. We lived in a rural area near many farms. We heard the sounds of night animals. The screech owls were very active and noisy.

Owls teach us several lessons to enhance of prayer life. These lessons help us enjoy prayer and to welcome God's Presence.

First of all, owls teach us not to be deterred by distractions. How many times have you prayed, only to be distracted. They remain focused when prey is spotted. Their eyes are glued to the target. We must keep our eyes on Jesus, and The Word of God.

Also, owls teach us about perspective. They have the ability to rotate their heads 270 degrees. They can look both forward and backward. I have witnessed this feat.

In order to make wise decisions, we must see what is in front of us, as well as what is behind us. Then we can make more informed decisions.

Listening skills is another valuable lesson. Owls sit quietly, and listen. They can detect a mouse about ¼ to ½ mile away. Scriptures encourage us to be still and to listen.

"Be still, and know that I am God; I will be exalted among the nations; I will be exalted in the earth." (Psalm 46:10)

Finally, of great significance, the owl sees in the dark of the night. Owls watch during the darkest of nights. They are alert and avert danger. Also, they see good things in the dark.

We need to look beyond a person's exterior and understand the conditions of the heart.

From darkness, we can spot hidden treasures, as we look with the eyes of The Spirit.

For these reasons the owl is the chosen symbol for the book, ASK, SEEK and KNOCK!

INTRODUCTION

"Ask and it will be given to you; seek and you will find; knock and the door will be opened to you. For everyone who asks receives; the one who seeks finds; and to the one who knocks, the door will be opened.

—Matthew 7:7-8 (NIV)

When speaking on prayer, Jesus tells us that we must *ask, seek, and knock*. Jesus' words describe the heart of a prayer life that is vibrant, persistent, and deeply connected to God. Prayer is not merely a ritual or a routine but an ongoing dialogue with God. It is through prayer that we discover the depths of God's love, the breadth of His wisdom, and the infinite reach of His power.

This book, *Ask, Seek, Knock*, will explore the progressive levels of prayer that Jesus teaches. Each level—asking, seeking, and knocking—carries its unique significance and power. By understanding and embracing these levels, we can strengthen our relationship with God and experience His presence in profound ways.

This book is a compact, easily accessible guide that you can carry with you, whether in your pocket, your bag, or your heart. It is designed to be a quick yet impactful read, perfect for those moments when you need encouragement, guidance, or a reminder of the power of prayer.

The inspiration behind this book comes from the desire to make prayer more approachable. Too often, we view prayer as a last resort rather than our first line of defense. We underestimate its power and, consequently, the connection it offers us with God. This book seeks to shift that perspective, presenting prayer as a progressive journey that begins with asking, deepens with seeking, and culminates in the transformative act of knocking.

Reading this Book

This book is divided into three main sections: **Ask**, **Seek**, and **Knock**. Each section delves into one of the progressive levels of prayer, offering biblical examples, principles, and practical applications.

1. Ask

In the first section, we explore what it means to ask in prayer. Jesus invites us to bring our needs, desires, and concerns to Him. Asking is about recognizing our dependence on

God and trusting in His provision. We will look at biblical examples such as the desperate leper who asked for healing and the persistent widow who sought justice. Through these stories, we learn the importance of humility, faith, and persistence when we come before God with our requests.

2. Seek

The second section takes us deeper into the act of seeking. Seeking goes beyond asking; it is about pursuing God's presence and His will for our lives. This kind of prayer is marked by a desire to know God more intimately and to align our hearts with His purposes. We will examine the lives of Elijah and Moses, who sought God with fervor and determination. Their stories reveal the transformative power of seeking God and the peace that comes from dwelling in His presence.

3. Knock

The final section focuses on knocking—prayer that demands an encounter with God. Knocking represents the bold and persistent pursuit of divine intervention. It is the kind of prayer that refuses to give up, even in the face of obstacles. We will look at the friends of the paralytic man and Blind Bartimaeus, who both demonstrated unwavering determination to reach Jesus. Their stories teach us about the importance of perseverance and the miraculous encounters that result from relentless faith.

Why This Book Matters

In today's fast-paced world, it's easy to feel disconnected from God. Our lives are filled with distractions, and our hearts often grow weary. Yet, prayer remains a powerful and accessible way to reconnect with the divine. By understanding and practicing the principles of asking, seeking, and knocking, we can experience a renewed sense of purpose and a deeper relationship with God.

This book is not just about learning new concepts; it's about transforming your prayer life. It's about discovering the joy of asking, the fulfillment of seeking, and the breakthroughs that come from knocking. Whether you are new to prayer or have been praying for years, this book offers insights and encouragement to take your prayer life to the next level.

As you journey through these pages, may you find inspiration, encouragement, and a renewed passion for prayer. Remember, God is always ready to listen. All we need to do is ask, seek, and knock.

CHAPTER 1: ASK

Jesus' invitation to ask is both simple and profound. When He says, "*Ask and keep on asking, and it will be given to you*," He opens the door for us to bring our needs, desires, and concerns directly to God. Asking in prayer is the first step in building a deeper relationship with our Creator. It's about recognizing our dependence on Him and trusting in His love and provision.

The Power of Asking

In the book of John, Jesus emphasizes the importance of asking when He says, "*Very truly I tell you, my Father will give you whatever you ask in my name*" (John 16:23, NIV). This promise is not a blank check for selfish desires but an invitation to align our requests with God's will and purpose. When we ask in Jesus' name, we are invoking His authority and acknowledging His lordship over our lives.

Asking is an act of faith. It demonstrates our belief that God is able and willing to intervene in our lives. It also shows our humility, as we admit our need for His help. This level of prayer is foundational, setting the stage for deeper levels of seeking and knocking.

Biblical Examples of Asking

The Desperate Leper

One of the most powerful examples of asking in prayer is found in the story of the desperate leper in Luke 5:12-13. The man, covered with leprosy, approached Jesus with a simple yet profound request: "*Lord, if you are willing, you can make me clean.*" His plea was born out of desperation and faith. He believed in Jesus' ability to heal but was unsure of His willingness.

Jesus' response was immediate and compassionate. He reached out His hand, touched the man, and said, "I am willing. Be clean!" Immediately, the leprosy left him. This story teaches us two important lessons: first, we must come to Jesus with our needs, and second, we must trust in His willingness to help us.

The Persistent Widow

Another powerful illustration of asking in prayer is the parable of the persistent widow in Luke 18:1-5. Jesus told this parable to His disciples to emphasize the importance of persistent prayer. In the story, a widow repeatedly approaches an unjust judge, pleading for justice against her adversary.

Despite the judge's reluctance, he eventually grants her request because of her persistence.

Jesus taught this parable to emphasize the importance of not giving up, but continuing to pray. The widow's relentless pursuit of justice mirrors our need to persist in prayer, even when answers seem delayed. God, unlike the unjust judge, is righteous and compassionate. He hears our prayers and responds in His perfect timing.

Principles of Asking in Prayer

Humility and Faith

When we come to God with our requests, we must do so with humility and faith. Humility acknowledges our dependence on God and recognizes that we cannot do it on our own. Faith, on the other hand, trusts in God's ability and willingness to meet our needs.

Jesus often highlighted the importance of faith in His teachings. In Matthew 21:22, He says, "*If you believe, you will receive whatever you ask for in prayer*" (NIV). This does not mean that we will always get exactly what we want, but it does mean that faith is a crucial component of effective prayer.

Aligning with God's Will

Asking in prayer also involves aligning our requests with God's will. In the book of 1 John, we read, "*This is the confidence we have in approaching God: that if we ask anything according to his will, he hears us. And if we know that he hears us—whatever we ask—we know that we have what we asked of him*" (1 John 5:14-15, NIV).

This passage reassures us that when our prayers align with God's will, He hears and answers them. Therefore, it is essential to seek God's will in our lives and align our desires with His purposes.

Application for Today

Bringing Our Needs to God

One of the most practical ways to apply the principle of asking in our daily lives is to bring our needs to God regularly. This can be done through personal prayer, journaling, or even sharing our requests with a trusted prayer partner. The act of verbalizing our needs to God helps to solidify our dependence on Him and opens the door for His intervention.

Persisting in Prayer

Persistence is key when it comes to asking in prayer. Just like the persistent widow, we must continue to bring our requests to God, even when answers seem delayed. This persistence demonstrates our faith and trust in God's timing and plan.

Practical Steps to Incorporate Asking in Prayer

1. **Set Aside Regular Prayer Time**: Dedicate specific times each day for prayer. Consistency is crucial in building a habit of asking.

2. **Be Specific in Your Requests**: When you pray, be specific about your needs and desires. This helps to clarify your intentions and align them with God's will.

3. **Keep a Prayer Journal**: Document your prayer requests and note how God answers them. This practice can strengthen your faith and provide encouragement over time.

4. **Pray with Others**: Engage in communal prayer with friends, family, or a prayer group. Collective prayer can be powerful and uplifting.

5. **Trust in God's Timing**:
   Understand that God's timing is
   perfect, even when it doesn't align
   with your expectations. Keep asking
   and trust that He is at work.

Hannah: A Mother's Prayer

In the book of 1 Samuel, we read the story
of Hannah, a woman deeply distressed by
her inability to conceive a child. In her
anguish, she prayed earnestly to the Lord,
asking for a son and vowing to dedicate him
to God's service. Her heartfelt plea did not
go unnoticed. God answered her prayer, and
she gave birth to Samuel, who would
become one of Israel's greatest prophets.

Hannah's story is a testament to the power
of earnest, heartfelt prayer. Her willingness
to pour out her soul before the Lord and her
faith in His ability to grant her request are
inspiring examples of what it means to ask
in prayer.

Asking in prayer is the foundation of a vibrant and dynamic relationship with God. It is an act of faith, humility, and trust. As we bring our needs to Him, we open the door for His blessings and intervention in our lives.

We must embrace the invitation to ask, knowing that our Heavenly Father delights in hearing and answering our prayers. As you cultivate a habit of asking, you will grow in faith, deepen your trust in God, and experience the abundant life He promises.

Reflection Questions:

1. What are some specific needs or desires that I have been hesitant to bring before God? Why?
2. How can I cultivate a habit of asking God for my needs with humility and faith?

3. In what ways have I seen God answer my prayers in the past, and how does that encourage me to ask boldly now?

Prayer: *Lord, I come to You with my needs and desires, trusting that You are willing and able to provide. Help me to ask with humility and faith, believing in Your goodness. Thank You for the ways You have answered my prayers in the past. Teach me to approach You boldly, knowing that You care for me deeply.*

CHAPTER 2: SEEK

While asking in prayer is about bringing our needs and desires before God, seeking goes deeper. Seeking involves a wholehearted pursuit of God's presence, His wisdom, and His will for our lives. Seeking transforms our prayer life from a list of requests to an ongoing relationship with our Creator.

The Power of Seeking

In Matthew 6:33, Jesus instructs, "*But seek first his kingdom and his righteousness, and all these things will be given to you as well*" (NIV). Seeking is about prioritizing God above all else. It is an intentional effort to align our hearts with His purposes and to grow in our understanding of who He is. When we seek God, we discover the fullness of His love, grace, and wisdom.

Seeking requires dedication and perseverance. It is a continuous journey where we learn to tune our hearts to His voice and to follow His guidance in every area of our lives.

Biblical Examples of Seeking

Elijah and the Prophets of Baal

One of the most dramatic examples of seeking God is found in the story of Elijah and the prophets of Baal in 1 Kings 18:20-40. During a time of spiritual decline in the nation of Israel, Elijah challenged the prophets of Baal. He issued a challenge to reveal that God was indeed the one True God, and Baal was a worthless idol.

1 Kings 18:21 reads, "*If the Lord is God, worship him! But if Baal is God, worship him. The people spoke not a word.*" The prophets of Baal spent hours calling on their god, but there was no response.

Elijah, on the other hand, sought the Lord with a sincere heart. He repaired the altar of the Lord and prayed a simple yet powerful prayer, asking God to reveal Himself so that the people would know that He alone is God. In response to Elijah's prayer, fire fell from heaven and consumed the sacrifice, the wood, the stones, and even the water in the trench around the altar.

Elijah's example teaches us that seeking God with a pure heart and a sincere desire for His glory can lead to powerful and miraculous outcomes. It shows us the importance of turning to God with our whole heart and trusting in His power.

Moses and the Tent of Meeting

Another profound example of seeking is found in the life of Moses. In Exodus 33:7-11, we read about Moses setting up a tent of meeting outside the camp, where he went to seek the Lord. Whenever Moses entered the tent, the pillar of cloud would descend and stand at the entrance while the Lord spoke with Moses face to face, as one speaks to a friend.

Moses' relationship with God was marked by intimacy and dedication. He sought God's presence continually, not just for guidance but for the sheer joy of being with Him. This deep and personal connection with God enabled Moses to lead the Israelites with wisdom and strength.

Moses' example challenges us to prioritize our relationship with God above all else. It encourages us to create spaces in our lives where we can meet with God regularly and seek His presence with all our hearts.

Principles of Seeking in Prayer

Sincerity and Dedication

Seeking God takes sincerity and dedication. It is about coming to God with an open heart and a genuine desire to know Him more. In Jeremiah 29:13, God promises, *"You will seek me and find me when you seek me with all your heart"* (NIV). This promise assures us that our efforts to seek God will not be in vain. When we approach Him with sincerity and dedication, He will reveal Himself to us.

Prioritizing God's Will

When we seek God, we prioritize His will above our own. Jesus modeled this in the Garden of Gethsemane when He prayed, *"My Father, if it is possible, may this cup be taken from me. Yet not as I will, but as you will*" (Matthew 26:39, NIV). Seeking God's will means surrendering our desires and submitting to His plans, trusting that His ways are higher and better than our own.

Application for Today

Cultivating a Habit of Seeking God

To incorporate the principle of seeking into our daily lives, we need to cultivate habits that draw us closer to God. This can include regular Bible study, prayer, worship, and quiet times of reflection. By intentionally setting aside time to seek God, we create opportunities for Him to speak to us and guide us.

Practical Steps to Develop a Habit of Seeking God

1. **Daily Devotionals**: Start each day with a time of devotion, reading Scripture, and reflecting on its

meaning. This sets the tone for seeking God throughout the day.

2. **Prayer Walks**: Take walks in nature or around your neighborhood, using the time to talk to God and listen for His voice.

3. **Journaling**: Keep a journal of your prayers, thoughts, and the ways you see God working in your life. This helps to document your journey and see patterns of His guidance.

4. **Worship and Praise**: Incorporate worship music into your daily routine. Singing praises to God can help you focus on His presence and goodness.

5. **Time for Stillness and Reflection**: When we pray, we must also take the time to listen. Just like any conversation, there is a time to talk and a time to listen. Spending time with God doesn't mean we have to

fill up the space with our own words; we also have to make the time to simply be in His presence and receive what He wishes to speak into our lives.

King David: A Heart After God

King David is often described as a man after God's own heart. Throughout the Psalms, we see his deep longing and earnest seeking of God. In Psalm 63:1, David writes, "*You, God, are my God, earnestly I seek you; I thirst for you, my whole being longs for you, in a dry and parched land where there is no water*" (NIV). David's life was marked by a passionate pursuit of God's presence, even amidst trials and challenges.

David's heart for God wasn't just revealed in his words, but also in his actions. One of the most powerful examples is when David inquired of the Lord before making important decisions. In 1 Samuel 23:2, when faced with the decision of whether or not to go into battle against the Philistines, David sought God's guidance: *"David inquired of the Lord, saying, 'Shall I go and attack these Philistines?' The Lord answered him, 'Go, attack the Philistines and save Keilah'"* (NIV).

This moment highlights David's dependence on God's wisdom rather than relying on his own understanding. He knew that victory, provision, and protection were found in seeking the Lord first. David's example reminds us to approach God in prayer, trusting that He is not only willing but ready to guide us in every step we take. Like David, we can have confidence that when we inquire of the Lord, He will respond with clarity and direction.

David's example inspires us to seek God earnestly, regardless of our circumstances. His psalms of praise, lament, and thanksgiving reflect a heart that constantly turned to God in every situation.

Seeking God is an inseparable part of the Christian life. Seeking moves us into a deeper relationship with our Creator. Through the examples of Elijah, Moses, and King David, we learn that seeking God requires sincerity, dedication, and a desire to prioritize His will above our own.

As we cultivate habits that draw us closer to God, we will experience the richness of His presence and the fullness of His guidance. We must embrace the call to seek God with all our hearts, knowing that He promises to be found by those who diligently pursue Him.

This journey of seeking will transform your prayer life and deepen your relationship with God. As you seek Him daily, you will discover the joy, peace, and strength that come from being in His presence.

Reflection Questions:

1. What steps can I take to prioritize seeking God's presence in my daily life?
2. How have I experienced God's guidance and peace when I have intentionally sought Him?
3. What areas of my life need to be more aligned with God's will and purposes?

Prayer: *Father, I long to know You more deeply and to seek Your presence above all else. Guide me as I pursue You, and help me to align my heart with Your will. Thank You for the peace and wisdom You provide when I seek You. Draw me closer to You each day, and let Your presence transform my life.*

Chapter 3: Knock

Knocking in prayer is the most determined and persistent form of seeking God. It is actively pursuing an encounter with Him and refusing to give up until that encounter happens. When Jesus says, "Knock and keep on knocking, and the door will be opened to you," He invites us to a level of intimacy with Him that demands attention, perseverance, and unwavering faith.

The Power of Knocking

Knocking is all about seeking a breakthrough. It is prayer that goes beyond asking and seeking to a point where we actively engage with God, expecting Him to respond. This form of prayer is an urgent and intense desire for God's intervention.

In Revelation 3:20, Jesus says, "*Here I am! I stand at the door and knock. If anyone hears my voice and opens the door, I will come in and eat with that person, and they with me*" (NIV). This verse shows the reciprocal nature of knocking: as we knock on God's door, He also knocks on the door of our hearts, inviting us into deeper relationship with Him.

Biblical Examples of Knocking

The Friends of the Paralytic

A powerful example of knocking in prayer is found in the story of the paralytic man and his friends in Mark 2:1-12. When Jesus returned to Capernaum, a large crowd gathered, making it impossible for the paralytic and his friends to reach Him through the door. Undeterred, they climbed onto the roof, created an opening, and lowered the man on a mat to where Jesus was teaching.

Their determination and faith attracted Jesus' attention. He saw their faith and said to the paralytic, "*Son, your sins are forgiven*" (Mark 2:5). Later, He healed the man, saying, "*I tell you, get up, take your mat and go home*" (Mark 2:11). This story illustrates the power of persistent, unwavering prayer that seeks an encounter with Jesus despite seemingly insurmountable obstacles.

Blind Bartimaeus

Another compelling example is Blind Bartimaeus in Mark 10:46-52. Bartimaeus, a blind beggar, sat by the roadside as Jesus was leaving Jericho. When he heard that Jesus was passing by, he began to shout, "*Jesus, Son of David, have mercy on me!*" Many in the crowd rebuked him and told him to be quiet, but Bartimaeus shouted all the more, "Son of David, have mercy on me!" (Mark 10:47-48). Despite being told to stay silent, he refused to give up, crying out even louder in his desperation to reach Jesus.

His persistence paid off. Jesus stopped and called him, asking, "*What do you want me to do for you?" Bartimaeus replied, "Rabbi, I want to see*" (Mark 10:51). Jesus said, "*Go, your faith has healed you*" (Mark 10:52). Immediately, he received his sight and followed Jesus along the road. Bartimaeus' story teaches us the importance of boldness and perseverance in prayer. When obstacles or discouragement arise, his example shows that our faith and persistence can draw the attention of Jesus, leading to powerful transformation.

Bartimaeus' encounter with Jesus not only demonstrates the power of persistence, but it also reveals the compassion of Christ. Though surrounded by a large crowd, Jesus noticed the cry of one man who refused to be silenced. He didn't see Bartimaeus as an interruption or a distraction but as a person in need of mercy. Jesus stopped, took the time to listen, and responded. This is a beautiful reminder that no matter how chaotic or crowded life may seem, God hears the cries of those who call out to Him in faith.

Bartimaeus' story challenges us to approach God with the same kind of boldness, knowing that He is attentive to every prayer. It also reminds us that when we refuse to let doubt or discouragement keep us from seeking Jesus, we open the door for God's transformative power to work in our lives. Through faith, persistence, and trust, just like Bartimaeus, we can experience breakthrough and healing.

Principles of Knocking in Prayer

Perseverance and Faith

Knocking in prayer requires perseverance and faith. It is about continuing to pray even when the answer is delayed or seems impossible. In Luke 11:9-10, Jesus says, "*So I say to you: Ask and it will be given to you; seek and you will find; knock and the door will be opened to you. For everyone who asks receives; the one who seeks finds; and to the one who knocks, the door will be opened*" (NIV). This passage encourages us to persist in prayer, trusting that God will answer in His perfect timing. Perseverance in prayer builds our faith and deepens our reliance on God.

However, sometimes delays are not just about timing, but about spiritual warfare. In Daniel 10:13, we see a striking example of this. Daniel had been praying for understanding, yet his answer seemed delayed. When the angel finally arrived, he revealed that he had been hindered by the "prince of the Persian kingdom" for 21 days. It wasn't until Michael, one of the chief princes, came to assist him that the angel could break through and deliver the message to Daniel. This passage provides a glimpse into the spiritual battles that can occur when we pray, reminding us that there are forces at work beyond what we can see.

Though it appeared as if God was slow to respond, the truth was that Daniel's prayers were heard from the moment he began. The delay wasn't a denial but a result of spiritual opposition. This encourages us to remain steadfast, knowing that our prayers are powerful and that sometimes the battle is happening in the unseen realms. Just like Daniel, we may not understand the full picture, but we can trust that God is always working on our behalf, and He will send help, just as He did with Michael. The key is to keep knocking, keep seeking, and trust that God is faithful to answer.

In Matthew 15:26, when Jesus says, "*It is not right to take the children's bread and toss it to the dogs*," He was responding to a Canaanite woman who came to Him, pleading for her daughter's healing. At first glance, this statement seems harsh, but it's important to understand the context. Jesus was initially sent to minister to the Jewish people, the "children" in this metaphor, as they were God's chosen people through whom salvation would come. The "bread" represents the blessings and healing that Jesus was bringing to them. The "dogs" were a common term used by Jews at the time to refer to Gentiles, indicating that they were outside the covenant promises.

However, this exchange reveals something deeper about Jesus' mission. When the woman responded in humility and faith, saying, "*Even the dogs eat the crumbs that fall from their master's table*" (Matthew 15:27), Jesus was moved by her great faith and granted her request. This story shows that Jesus' ministry was not limited by cultural or ethnic boundaries. Though He came first for the Jews, His mercy and grace extended beyond them to anyone who had faith. The conversation demonstrates that, while the timing of His ministry was specific, God's heart is for all people, and faith.

Expecting a Breakthrough

When we knock in prayer, we should do so with an expectation of breakthrough. James 1:6-7 says, "*But when you ask, you must believe and not doubt, because the one who doubts is like a wave of the sea, blown and tossed by the wind. That person should not expect to receive anything from the Lord*" (NIV). Expecting a breakthrough means approaching God with confidence, believing that He is able and willing to intervene in our circumstances.

Application for Today

Pursuing Persistent Prayer

To apply the principle of knocking, we need to develop a habit of persistent prayer. We must set aside dedicated times for prayer, as well as be mindful of opportunities to pray throughout the day. Persistent prayer means we consistently bring our requests before God and refuse to give up, even when answers seem delayed.

Practical Steps to Practice Knocking in Prayer

1. **Set Specific Prayer Goals**: Identify specific areas in your life where you need a breakthrough and commit to praying persistently for them.
2. **Create a Prayer Routine**: Establish a routine that includes regular times

of prayer. Consistency is key in developing perseverance.

3. **Join a Prayer Group**: Engaging with a community of believers who are also committed to persistent prayer can provide support and encouragement.

4. **Use Prayer Prompts**: Utilize prayer prompts or lists to help focus your prayers and ensure you cover all areas of concern.

5. **Celebrate Small Victories**: Acknowledge and celebrate small answers to prayer as they come. This builds faith and encourages continued persistence.

Encouraging Stories of Knocking

The Syrophoenician Woman

In Matthew 15:21-28, we find the story of the Syrophoenician woman who came to

Jesus, pleading for her demon-possessed daughter to be healed. Initially, Jesus did not answer her, and His disciples urged Him to send her away. But the woman persisted, even when Jesus said that His mission was first to the lost sheep of Israel.

Undeterred, she knelt before Him and said, *"Lord, help me!"* Jesus replied, *"It is not right to take the children's bread and toss it to the dogs."* She responded, *"Yes it is, Lord. Even the dogs eat the crumbs that fall from their master's table."* Jesus, moved by her faith and persistence, said, *"Woman, you have great faith! Your request is granted."* And her daughter was healed at that moment.

This story demonstrates the power of persistent, faith-filled prayer, even in the face of initial rejection.

The Early Church

In Acts 12:1-17, we read about Peter's miraculous escape from prison. King Herod had arrested Peter and intended to bring him to trial after Passover. While Peter was in prison, the church prayed earnestly to God for him. The night before his trial, an angel of the Lord appeared, and Peter's chains fell off. The angel led him out of the prison, past the guards, and through the iron gate that led to the city.

The church's persistent prayers resulted in a miraculous intervention. This account encourages us to persist in prayer, even when the situation seems dire or hopeless.

Knocking in prayer means actively pursuing an encounter with God, expecting a breakthrough, and refusing to give up. Through the examples of the friends of the paralytic, Blind Bartimaeus, the Syrophoenician woman, and the early church, we learn that persistent, faith-filled prayer can lead to miraculous outcomes.

As we develop a habit of knocking in prayer, we need to approach God with confidence and perseverance. Trust in His timing, expect His intervention, and remain steadfast in your pursuit of His presence. Knocking on God's door with faith and determination opens the way for transformative encounters and profound breakthroughs in our lives and faith.

This journey of knocking will transform your prayer life and deepen your relationship with God. Knock daily and discover the power, peace, and joy that come from persistent and faith-filled prayer.

Reflection Questions:

1. What situations in my life require persistent and determined prayer for breakthrough?
2. How can I strengthen my perseverance in prayer, even when answers seem delayed?

3. In what ways have I witnessed
    God's miraculous interventions in
    response to persistent prayer?

Prayer: *Lord, I come before You, knocking with faith and determination for the breakthroughs I need. Strengthen my perseverance in prayer, and remind me that Your timing is perfect. Thank You for the ways You have moved miraculously in my life. I trust in Your power and Your willingness to open doors that seem closed.*

CONCLUSION

As we journey through the principles of asking, seeking, and knocking in prayer, we uncover the profound depth and power that a committed prayer life can bring. Each level of prayer—asking, seeking, and knocking—invites us into a deeper relationship with God, where our faith is strengthened, our hearts are aligned with His will, and our lives are transformed by His presence.

Asking is the foundation of prayer. It is where we present our needs, desires, and concerns to God, recognizing our dependence on His provision. Through the examples of the desperate leper and the persistent widow, we learn the importance of humility, faith, and perseverance when bringing our requests to God. We are encouraged to boldly approach the throne of grace, trusting that our Heavenly Father hears and responds to our prayers.

Seeking takes us deeper, moving beyond our needs to a heartfelt pursuit of God's presence and His will. The stories of Elijah and Moses illustrate the power of seeking God with sincerity and dedication. Seeking involves prioritizing God above all else, desiring to know Him more intimately, and aligning our hearts with His purposes. As we seek God, we experience the richness of His presence and the fullness of His guidance.

Knocking represents the most determined and persistent form of prayer. It is about actively pursuing an encounter with God and refusing to give up until that encounter is realized. Through the examples of the friends of the paralytic, Blind Bartimaeus, and the Syrophoenician woman, we learn the importance of perseverance and unwavering faith. Knocking on God's door with faith and determination opens the way for miraculous interventions and profound breakthroughs.

The journey of prayer is a lifelong adventure. It is an invitation to continually grow in our relationship with God, to deepen our trust in Him, and to experience His love and power in ever-increasing measure. As we embrace the principles of asking, seeking, and knocking, we position ourselves to receive all that God has for us.

Remember, prayer is not just about changing our circumstances; it is about changing us. It shapes our character, molds our hearts, and aligns our desires with God's will. Through prayer, we become more like

Jesus, reflecting His love, grace, and wisdom to the world around us.

As we wrap up our time together, I challenge you to deepen your prayer life. Embrace the practice of asking, seeking, and knocking with renewed fervor and commitment. Here are a few practical steps to help you along the way:

1. **Make Prayer a Priority**: Set aside dedicated times each day for prayer. Create a quiet space where you can meet with God regularly and without distractions.

2. **Be Specific and Bold in Your Requests**: Don't hesitate to bring your needs and desires to God. Be specific in your prayers and trust that He is able and willing to respond.

3. **Pursue God's Presence**: Seek God not just for what He can do for you,

but for who He is. Spend time in worship, meditation, and reflection, desiring to know Him more deeply.

4. **Persist in Prayer**: When answers seem delayed, don't give up. Keep knocking with faith and determination, believing that God's timing is perfect.

5. **Join a Community of Prayer**: Engage with others who are committed to prayer. Join a prayer group, attend prayer meetings, and encourage one another in your spiritual journeys. This is great in-person, but can also be by phone, online, etc.

As you live out these practices, may you experience the transformative power of prayer in your life. May you grow in faith, deepen your relationship with God, and witness His miraculous work in and through you.

Closing Prayer

Heavenly Father, we thank You for the gift of prayer. We thank You for the promise that when we ask, seek, and knock, You hear us and respond. Help us to grow in our prayer lives, to seek You with all our hearts, and to persist in faith. May our prayers align with Your will and bring glory to Your name. We ask for Your guidance, strength, and wisdom as we continue this journey of prayer. In Jesus' name, Amen.

www.ingramcontent.com/pod-product-compliance
Lightning Source LLC
Chambersburg PA
CBHW060353130626
46553CB00003B/1207